INCA path

Dafne Arlman

For my little prince Tycho

COVER When you bloom like a flower, the Hummingbird will
come to drink your nectar. You will become a total healer.

Andean Tradition

The Andean tradition is a way of knowledge that incorporates nature as a whole of which we are all part and that is part of us. You learn how to communicate and relate directly with the world of living energies. Recognizing this spirit in each of the animate and inanimate beings with whom life is integrated.

Juan Nuñez del Prado is an anthropologist and a fourth level teacher in the Andean tradition. Juan has studied this tradition since 1968 and has trained with Q'ero priests. His father, anthropologist Oscar Nuñez del Prado, 'discovered' the Q'ero Indians - direct descendants of the Incas - in 1949 and led the first expedition to their villages in 1955.

Inca path 1 - The right side

Lessons from Don Juan Nuñez del Prado, his son Don Ivan and master Don Benito Qoriwaman.

The right side of the sacred path is about the mythical aspect of daily life. Like an Inca you learn how to communicate and relate directly with the world of living energies. The lessons are about relationships between your energetic bubble and the bubble of others.

There exist a living energy (Kausay), which is made up of two different forces: light energy (sami) and heavy energy (hucha). This path will teach you how to move the kausay for the good of others.

OPEN YOUR FONTANEL AND LET IN

YOUR HEAVY ENERGY TO MOTHER EARTH

02 2009

THE FINE ENERGY OF FATHER COSMOS   AND LET GO

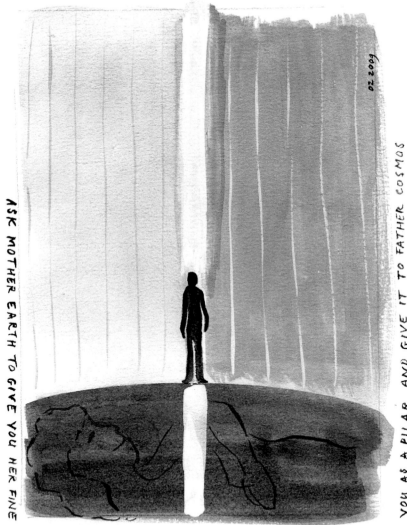

DZ 2009

ASK MOTHER EARTH TO GIVE YOU HER FINE

YOU AS A PILAR AND GIVE IT TO FATHER COSMOS

ENERGY THROUGH YOUR FEET LET IT STREAM THROUGH

Huchamijuy

02 2009

OPEN YOUR QOSQO, YOUR SPIRITUAL

STOMACH EAT THE HEAVY ENERGY OF SOME ONE

AND DIGEST BY SEPARATING IT IN TWO STREAMS

Misha Chakuy

I RECEIVE AN INITIATION OF MY INKAMASTER WITH HIS MESA. I FEEL CONNECTED TO THE LINE OF MASTERS FROM THE ANDES

Pocpo

LIVING ENERGY IS EVERYWHERE

I CONNECT WITH THE BUBBLE OF A TREE AND

WITH THE BUBBLE OF A LITTLE LAKE

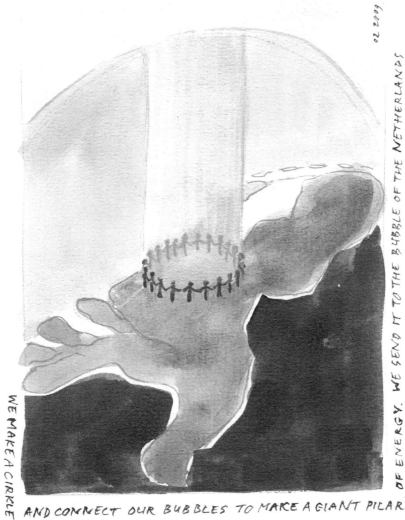

02.2009

WE MAKE A CIRKLE

AND CONNECT OUR BUBBLES TO MAKE A GIANT PILAR

OF ENERGY. WE SEND IT TO THE BUBBLE OF THE NETHERLANDS

Inca path 2 - The middle side

Lessons from Don Juan Nuñez del Prado, his son Don Ivan and master Don Andres Espinoza.

The middle side of the sacred path is about the space in your own energetic bubble (pocpo). You learn how to open the seven energetic eyes (nawi), make five energetic belts (chumpi) and clean your connections. Visualising your conception and death is an exploration of your spiritual self.

In the Andean tradition it is noble to develop your personal capacity and use it in your community. This path will strenghten your autonomy so that you will be courageous to be yourself within your community.

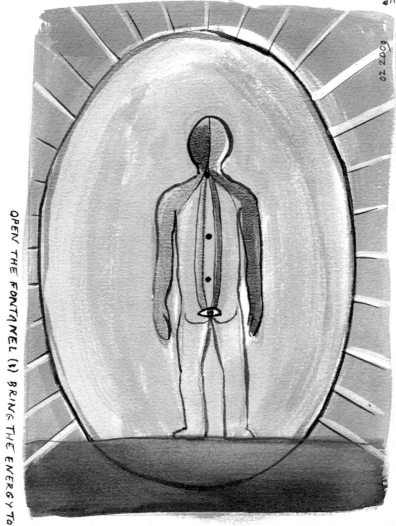

02 2009

OPEN THE FONTANEL (↓) BRING THE ENERGY TO

BRING A SILVER AND GOLDEN CORD TILL THE TAILBONE. OPEN IT AND BRING GREEN

THE CROWN AND THEN DOWN TILL THE NECK. TWIST AND

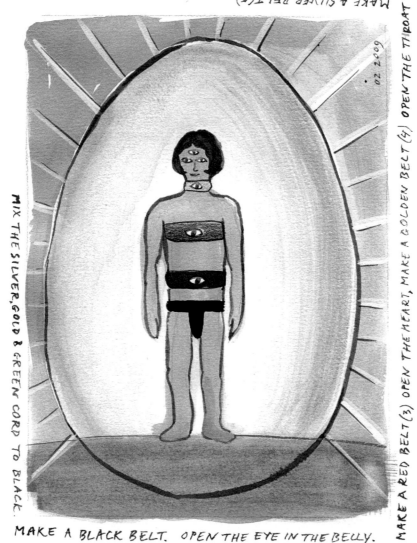

MIX THE SILVER, GOLD & GREEN CORD TO BLACK.

MAKE A SILVER BELT(5) OPEN THE THROAT

02 2009

MAKE A RED BELT (3) OPEN THE HEART, MAKE A GOLDEN BELT (4)

MAKE A BLACK BELT. OPEN THE EYE IN THE BELLY.

PULL THE ENERGY TO THE CHIN, MOUTH, NOSE.

THIRD EYE. FILL YOURSELF WITH PURPLE LIGHT. CORDS BREAK UP.

OPEN THE RIGHT EYE. OPEN THE LEFT EYE. OPEN THE

Munay Muyu

WE STAND

BACK TO BACK AND MAKE A VERTIKAL CIRKLE OF ENERGY TROUGH THE SPINE

Munay Muyu

WE STAND

FRONT TO FRONT AND MAKE A HORIZONTAL CIRKLE OF

ENERGY. WE CONNECT OUR 6 EYES

02 2009

Munay Muyu

02 2009

ROUND IN HORIZONTAL AND VERTICAL CIRKLES, LIKE A CHAIN

WE MAKE A CIRKLE BACK TO BACK FRONT TO FRONT. WE MAKE THE ENERGY GO

I GO BACK IN MY MEMORIES AND CLEAN ALL HEAVY ENERGY UNTIL MY CONCEPTION. I INVITE MY PARENTS TO DO THE SAME. AS I ENCLOSE THEM IN MY HEART, A BUTTERFLY APPEARS

02 2009

I LOOK FORWARD TO THE MOMENT I WILL DIE

TO SAY GOOD-BYE. MY MOTHER IS THERE TO BRING ME HOME

I AM IN THE HAGUE AND MY FRIENDS AND FAMILY COME

Spiral

WE MAKE A SPIRAL OF MEN AND WOMEN. WE WALK CLOCKWISE AROUND EACH OTHER. IT MAKES ME VERY LOVELY....

Inca path 3 - The left side

Lessons from Don Juan Nuñez del Prado, his son Don Ivan and master Don Melchor Deza.

The left side is the magic and intuitive side of the sacred path. You learn how to deal with the power within you and how to cooperate with your eight allies. You will use the power of language, dance, knowledge, affection and impulses.

The inca seed, your personal capacity, will be activated to develop into the highest spiritual level. This path stimulates the development of your own unique individual potential in your own truth.

I CLEAN MY THREE EYES AND I INVITE MY HELPERS TO COME IN. I CAN SEE THEM ONE BY ONE

Munay

02 2009

I CLEAN MY INKASEED AND I INVITE MY HELPERS TO COME IN. I EMBRACE MY HEART AND IT BECOMES SO BIG TO LOVE

Tarpuy

I BRING MY INKASEED DOWN TO

MY TAIL BONE AND PLANT IT IN MOTHER EARTH

MY HELPERS ARE SO ENTHUSIASTIC THEY DANCE

02 2009

Mallki

J BRING FINE ENERGY OF MOTHER EARTH AROUND ME AND THROUGH ALL MY EYES IN MY SPINE. SLOWLY A BIG TREE GROWS AROUND ME

Qanchis Poqpo

I BRING FINE ENERGY OF MOTHER EARTH THROUGH ALL MY EYES IN MY SPINE

IT GIVES ME POWER TO ENLARGE MY BUBBLE IN 7 LAYERS

02 2009

Tawantin

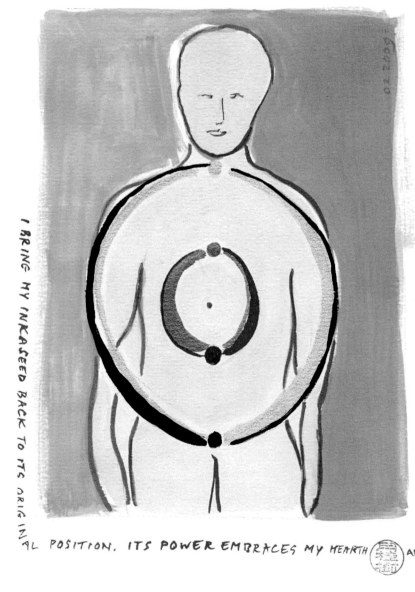

I BRING MY INKASEED BACK TO ITS ORIGINAL POSITION. ITS POWER EMBRACES MY HEARTH AND MY BELLY AND MY THROAT AND TAIL

Amaru

02.2009

I INVITE MY ANACONDA TO COME. SEEING HER GIVES ME POWER

I BRING FINE ENERGY OF MOTHER EARTH THROUGH 4 EYES UP TO THE SPINE

Inca path 4 - Masterclass

Lessons from Don Juan Nuñez del Prado,
his son Don Ivan and master Don Tata
Lorenzo from Bolivia.

The masterclass will profound your
knowledge of the Andean Tradition.
You learn different healing techniques.

This class teaches you more about the levels
of consciousness. The fourth level makes a
connection with the world, the fifth with
the stars, the sixth with the Galaxy and the
seventh with the Universe. The connection
between the Andean tradition and Jung and
archetypes is made.

Wasi

EVERYONE HAS THREE HOUSES:

THE FIRST ONE IS YOUR OWN BUBBLE, THE SECOND IS

THE BUBBLE OF YOUR FAMILY, THE THIRD ONE IS THE BUBBLE OF YOUR NATION

P'ichay

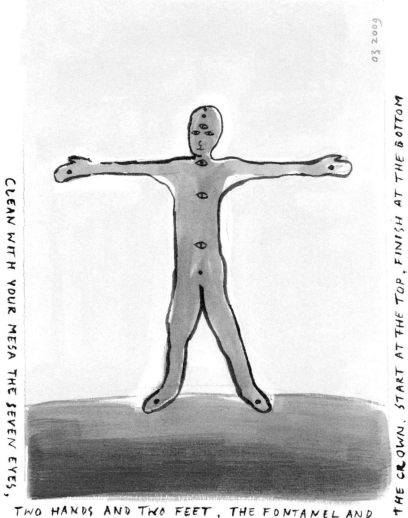

03 2009

CLEAN WITH YOUR MESA THE SEVEN EYES,

THE CROWN, START AT THE TOP, FINISH AT THE BOTTOM

TWO HANDS AND TWO FEET, THE FONTANEL AND

MAKE SEVEN CONNECTIONS : YOUR CROWN WITH THE COSMOS, YOUR FEET WITH THE EARTH, YOUR LEFT HAND WITH YOUR FAMILY, YOUR RIGHT WITH YOUR NATION, YOUR FRONT WITH THE PAST, YOUR BACK WITH THE FUTURE, YOUR HEART WITH HERE AND NOW.

Tarpuy

03 2009

EARTH.

WORLD. THEN BRING IT TO YOUR BELLY, TO YOUR TAILBONE AND TO THE

BRING YOUR INKASEED UP TO YOUR HEART

THEN TO YOUR THROAT, TO YOUR HEAD AND TO THE UPPER

PULL UP MIX OF ENERGY FROM SEED AND MOTHER

SOLID IRON STICK. EXPLODE IN 4 DIRECTIONS.

03 2009

EARTH. RECOVER YOUR AXIS UNTIL YOU FEEL A

GO TO THE MOMENT OF DEATH. GIVE YOUR BODY TO MOTHER EARTH. OFFER YOUR ANCHORS TO THE COLLECTIVE SOUL. FOLLOW YOUR SPIRIT TO HEAVEN. PUT YOUR SEED IN YOUR BODY.

03 2009

THE ROYAL COUPLE IS A MARRIAGE

WITH HIS WITCH, THE BUBBLE WILL MERGE

BETWEEN A WOMAN AND HER NEANDERTHAD AND A MAN

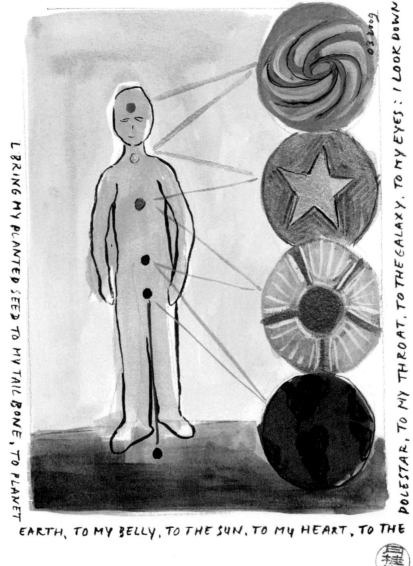

Willka Muju

I BRING MY PLANTED SEED TO MY TAIL BONE, TO PLANET EARTH, TO MY BELLY, TO THE SUN, TO MY HEART, TO THE POLESTAR, TO MY THROAT, TO THE GALAXY, TO MY EYES: I LOOK DOWN AT THE GALAXY.

Soqtantin

03 2009

WE MAKE AN AXIS IN THE MIDDLE OF

AND DANCE AS CHILDREN OF THE GALAXY

TWO TRIANGLES, ONE MALE AND ONE FEMALE. WE MOVE

RELATED WEBSITES
www.tawantin.com
www.tawantin.nl
www.inka-online.com
www.inkaspirit.nl
www.inkaspirit.com

RELATED BOOKS
Return of the Inka
By Elizabeth B. Jenkins
Journey to Q'eros: Golden Cradle of the Inka
By Elizabeth B. Jenkins
'Het Geheim van de Inca,' de lessen van de keizer
Achtergronden Profetie en Toepassingen
By Marie Louise Ambrosius

Made in the USA
San Bernardino, CA
23 May 2017